Our Amazing Universe -- through the lens of the historic Hubble Space Telescope

"All About This & That" Picture Book Series for Children (Volume 2)

By Adrian D. Robbe

Note: *Our Amazing Universe* -- "All About This & That" Picture Book Series for Children (Volume 2) is neither authorized nor endorsed (explicitly or implicitly) by the National Aeronautics and Space Administration (NASA) or the Space Telescope Science Institute (STScI).

Photo Credits: Front cover image of "Westerlund 2 Star Cluster" is from NASA. Photo credit for back cover of "Shuttle Servicing Mission 1 [SM1] for Hubble Space Telescope" is from NASA. Background image of "Stars in Night Sky" was obtained from Pixabay, is free of copyright, and is released under the Creative Commons License CC0 into the public domain. Photo credits for all other pictures used within this book are cited underneath each image, as appropriate.

First Edition: 2017

Printed in the United States of America

ISBN 978-1-520-98614-2

Distribution Platform/Publisher of Record: Createspace, a DBA of On-Demand Publishing, LLC, an Amazon company.

Outline

The pictures presented in this book are about the following topics:

Concept of a Space-Based Telescope

How did the concept of a space-based telescope actually begin?

Photo Credit: Pixabay

In 1946, physicist and astronomer Lyman Spitzer proposed the idea that a large space-based telescope "would not suffer from the blurring effects of Earth's atmosphere."[1] He believed that a spaced-based observatory would reveal much clearer images than any ground-based telescope"[2] on Earth.

The Journey Begins

What agencies were the first to be involved in exploring the concept of a space-based telescope?

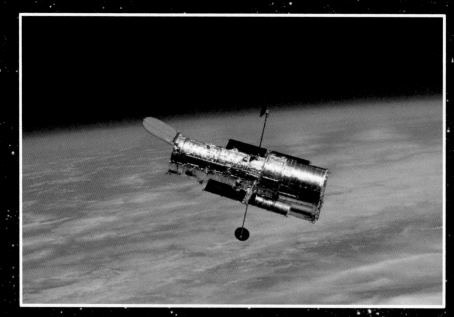

Photo Credit: NASA

In 1976, the European Space Agency (ESA) partnered with America's National Aeronautics and Space Administration (NASA) to support science operations in support of Spitzer's space telescope concept.[3] The following year in 1977, "Congress subsequently authorized the visionary mission"[4] for development and operation of a telescope in outer space.

Hubble Space Telescope

When did the dream of a space-based telescope become a reality?

Photo Credit: NASA

Photo Credit: NASA

Thirteen years later on April 25, 1990, the dream of having a working telescope in space became a reality when the astronauts assigned to the Space Shuttle *Discovery* STS-31 mission successfully deployed the Hubble Space Telescope into orbit.[5] "About the size of a large school bus"[6], the Hubble Space Telescope "filled the payload bay of the Space Shuttle *Discovery*"[7] when it was carried and then released into space "to begin its journey of discovery."[8]

Hubble's Challenges

What problem occurred with the Hubble Space Telescope after it was released into orbit?

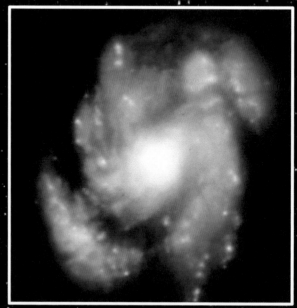

Photo Credit: NASA

Hubble was successfully placed "into orbit hundreds of miles above the ground."[9] However, "despite the promise of remarkable pictures due to its position above Earth's atmosphere, Hubble's operation started dismally."[10] "Instead of crisp, point-like images of stars, astronomers saw stars surrounded by large, fuzzy halos of light. The problem was… [due to] the edges of Hubble's large, primary mirror… [being] ground too flat by just a fraction of the width of a human hair."[11]

Travail Turns into Triumph

Before SM1   After SM1

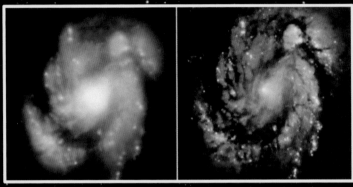

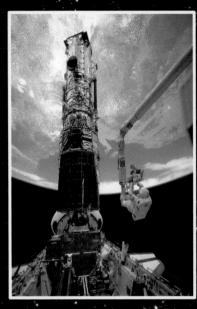

Photo Credit: NASA

Photo Credit: NASA

Shuttle "Servicing Mission 1 [SM1], launched in December 1993, was the first opportunity to conduct planned maintenance on the telescope."[12] "New instruments were installed and the optics of the flaw in Hubble's primary mirror was corrected."[13] The above two images "of the galaxy M100 shows the dramatic improvement in Hubble Space Telescope's view… after the first servicing mission [SM1]"[14] was complete.

A Highly Successful Science Program

"Hubble is now functioning at its peak scientific performance."[17]

Photo Credit: NASA, ESA, and The Hubble Heritage Team (STScI/AURA)

"Following its launch [in 1990], Hubble was repaired, maintained, and upgraded by astronauts five times over a period of 19 years."[15] The servicing missions provided by NASA's Space Shuttle astronauts have upgraded Hubble's "computers, mechanisms, and instruments... [and] have kept the observatory at the forefront of discovery by providing it with increasingly sensitive and accurate components."[16]

Hubble's Spectacular Pictures

View of the Hubble
Space Telescope
in orbit above the
planet Earth.

Photo Credit: NASA

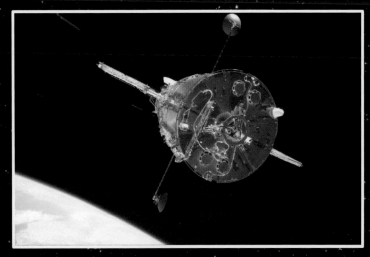

Photo Credit: NASA

    Spectacular pictures from Hubble are shown in the remaining pages of this book. The images are a vivid testimony of just a 'few of the amazing discoveries' that have been made through the historic Hubble Space Telescope. As you look at these magnificent images, you will be inspired by the awesome wonder of the universe that surrounds us. Hubble's scientific observations are truly amazing!

Mystic Mountain in Carina Nebula

Photo Credit: NASA, ESA, and M. Livio and the
Hubble 20th Anniversary Team (STScI)

Note: A nebula is a cloud of gas that occurs between stars in space.

Hodge 301 Star Cluster

Photo Credit: NASA

Note: A star cluster is a group of stars in outer space.

Monkey Head Nebula

Photo Credit: NASA, ESA, and The Hubble Heritage Team (STScI/AURA)

Horsehead Nebula

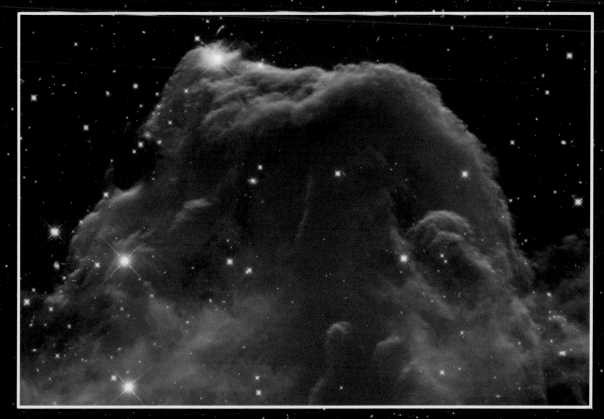

Photo Credit: NASA, ESA, and The Hubble Heritage Team (STScI/AURA)

M16 (Eagle Nebula)

Photo Credit: NASA, ESA, and The Hubble Heritage Team (STScI/AURA)

Note: Named after the French Astronomer Charles Messier, the letter "M" stands for a Messier space object.

NGC 2207 and IC 2163

Photo Credit: NASA

Note: NGC 2207 is the larger galaxy on left; IC 2163 is the smaller galaxy on the right.
NGC stands for New General Catalogue (NGC), a list of known galaxies, nebula, and stars
in deep space. IC stands for Index Catalogue (IC), an additional list of deep space objects.

Carina Nebula NGC 3372

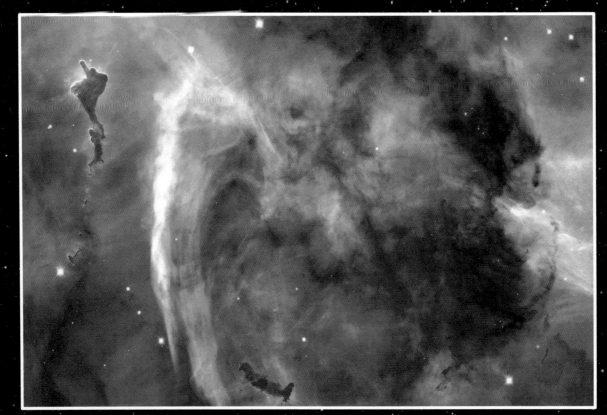

Photo Credit: NASA

Galaxy NGC 4214

Photo Credit: NASA

Note: A galaxy is a large system of stars in outer space.

Orion Nebula NGC 1976

Photo Credit: NASA

Bubble Nebula NGC 7635

Photo Credit: NASA, ESA, and The Hubble Heritage Team (STScI/AURA)

Spiral Galaxy NGC 4603

Photo Credit: NASA

Quintuplet Star Cluster

Photo Credit: NASA

Galaxy NGC 4414

Photo Credit: NASA

Red Supergiant Star

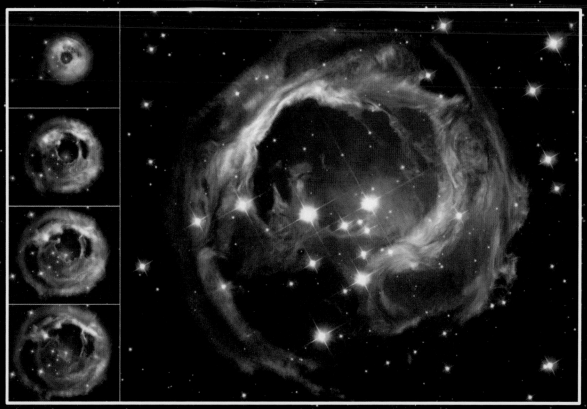

Photo Credit: NASA, ESA, and The Hubble Heritage Team (STScI/AURA)

Galaxy Pair Arp 273

Photo Credit: NASA, ESA, and The Hubble Heritage Team (STScI/AURA)

Note: The larger galaxy at the top is UGC 1810; the smaller galaxy below it is UGC 1813.

M80 Star Cluster

Photo Credit: NASA

Westerlund 2 Star Cluster

Photo Credit: NASA

Mars... the Red Planet

Photo Credit: NASA

Bok Globules in NGC 281

Photo Credit: NASA, ESA, and The Hubble Heritage Team (STScI/AURA)

28   Note: Bok Globules are dark cloud-like formations of dust and gas in outer space.

Spiral Galaxy NGC 3370

Photo Credit: NASA, The Hubble Heritage Team and A. Riess (STScI)

Bug Nebula NGC 6302

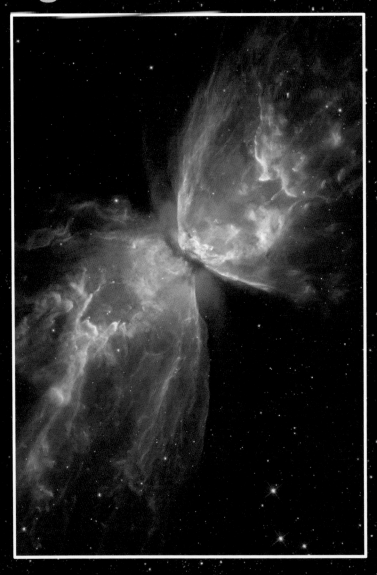

Photo Credit: NASA, ESA, and The Hubble SM4 ERO Team

Spiral Galaxy NGC 2841

Photo Credit: NASA, ESA, and The Hubble Heritage Team (STScI/AURA)-ESA/ Hubble Collaboration

Stellar Spire in Eagle Nebula

Photo Credit: NASA, ESA, and The
Hubble Heritage Team (STScI/AURA)

Spiral Galaxy NGC 1300

Photo Credit: NASA, ESA, and The Hubble Heritage Team (STScI/AURA)

Omega Centauri

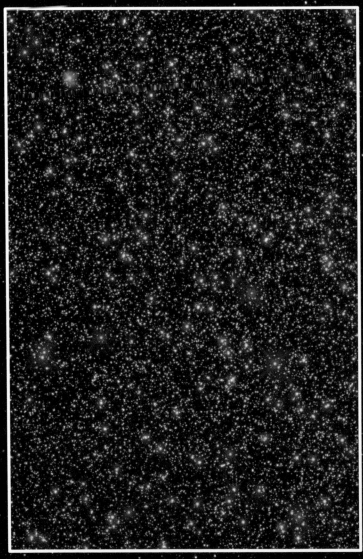

Photo Credit: NASA, ESA, and The Hubble SM4 ERO Team

Pinwheel-Shaped Galaxy NGC 1309

Photo Credit: NASA, ESA, The Hubble Heritage Team, (STScI/AURA) and A. Riess (STScI)

Sombrero Galaxy M104

Photo Credit: NASA and The Hubble Heritage Team (STScI/AURA)

Jet in Carina

Photo Credit: NASA, ESA, and The Hubble SM4 ERO Team

Whirlpool Galaxy M51

Photo Credit: NASA, ESA, S. Beckwith (STScI), and The Hubble Heritage Team (STScI/AURA)

Stephan's Quintet

Photo Credit: NASA, ESA, and The Hubble SM4 ERO Team

Magellanic Cloud NGC 346

Photo Credit: NASA, ESA, and A. Nota (STScI/ESA)

Try to match the names with the pictures that you learned about in *Our Amazing Universe*.

Monkey Head Nebula (page 12)

Horsehead Nebula (page 13)

M16 (Eagle Nebula) (page 14)

Bubble Nebula NGC 7635 (page 19)

Galaxy Pair Arp 273 (page 24)

Westerlund 2 Star Cluster (page 26)

Bug Nebula NGC 6302 (page 30)

Stellar Spire in Eagle Nebula (page 32)

Spiral Galaxy NGC 1300 (page 33)

Sombrero Galaxy M104 (page 36)

Jet in Carina (page 37)

Magellanic Cloud NGC 346 (page 40)

Footnote References

1. National Aeronautics and Space Administration (NASA). *Hubble: An Overview of the Space Telescope*. Hubble's History, p. 9. Edited by K. Hartnett and J. Jeletic. NASA's Goddard Space Flight Center, Greenbelt, Maryland: NASA Pub. 2013-07-032-GSFC, 2013. 66 pp.

2. NASA. *Hubble: An Overview of the Space Telescope*, Hubble's History, p. 9.

3. NASA. *Hubble: An Overview of the Space Telescope*, Hubble's History, p. 9.

4. NASA. *Hubble: An Overview of the Space Telescope*, Hubble's History, p. 9.

5. NASA. *Hubble: An Overview of the Space Telescope*, Hubble's History, p. 10.

6. NASA. *Hubble: An Overview of the Space Telescope*, Observatory Design, p. 23.

7. NASA. *Hubble: An Overview of the Space Telescope*, Observatory Design, p. 23.

8. NASA. *Hubble: An Overview of the Space Telescope*, Hubble's History, p. 11.

9. National Aeronautics and Space Administration (NASA). *Hubble 25: A Quarter-Century of Discovery with the Hubble Space Telescope*. 25 Years of Hubble, p. 4. Publication date: April 24, 2015. 99 pp.

10. NASA. *Hubble: An Overview of the Space Telescope*, Hubble's History, p. 12.

11. NASA. *Hubble: An Overview of the Space Telescope*, Hubble's History, p. 12.

12. NASA website. *Hubble Space Telescope: Servicing Missions, SM1 (Shuttle Endeavour Mission STS-61): Dec. 2-13, 1993*. Retrieved on 28 March 2017 from https://asd.gsfc.nasa.gov/archive/hubble/missions/sm1.html

13. NASA website. *Hubble Space Telescope: Servicing Missions, SM1 (Shuttle Endeavour Mission STS-61): Dec. 2-13, 1993*. Retrieved on 28 March 2017 from https://asd.gsfc.nasa.gov/archive/hubble/missions/sm1.html

14. NASA website. *Hubble Space Telescope: Hubble Servicing Missions Overview.* Retrieved on 28 March 2017 from https://www.nasa.gov/mission_pages/hubble/servicing/index.html

15. NASA. *Hubble: An Overview of the Space Telescope*, Hubble's History, p. 13.

16. NASA. *Hubble: An Overview of the Space Telescope*, Observatory Design, p. 23.

Sources of Research

Narrative Text Credits: The narrative texts used in writing *Our Amazing Universe* -- "All About This & That" Picture Book Series for Children (Volume 2) are based on material created, authored, and/or prepared by the Space Telescope Science Institute (STScI) for the National Aeronautics and Space Administration (NASA) under Contract NAS5-26555. All STScI informational material used in *Our Amazing Universe* is appropriately acknowledged in the footnote references section of this book. The STScI sources of reference include the following two ebooks that are available through the HubbleSite eBook Library web page -- http://hubble.stsci.edu/ebooks

1. **National Aeronautics and Space Administration**. *Hubble: An Overview of the Space Telescope*. Edited by K. Hartnett and J. Jeletic. NASA's Goddard Space Flight Center, Greenbelt, Maryland: NASA Pub. 2013-07-032-GSFC, 2013. 66 pp. This book is a joint project of NASA's Goddard Space Flight Center and the Space Telescope Science Institute under contract NAS5-26555.

2. **National Aeronautics and Space Administration**. *Hubble 25: A Quarter-Century of Discovery with the Hubble Space Telescope*. Publication date: April 24, 2015. 99 pp. This book is a joint project of NASA's Goddard Space Flight Center and the Space Telescope Science Institute under contract NAS5-26555.

Note: As explained on the internet STScI HubbleSite, no claim to copyright is asserted by STScI for information credited to them and may be freely used as in the public domain in accordance with NASA's contract. For further information, see the HubbleSite copyright page at http://hubble.stsci.edu/about_us/copyright.php

Photo Credits: The images used in *Our Amazing Universe* – "All About This & That" Picture Book Series for Children (Volume 2) were excerpted from NASA's Hubble Space Telescope image album archives posted in the "NASA on The Commons" Flickr web page as well as the "Astronomy Printshop Image Gallery in the Space Telescope Science Institute (STScI) HubbleSite. Details concerning the source of these images are as follows:

1. **NASA on The Commons**, Hubble Space Telescope Album, Flickr website -- https://www.flickr.com/photos/nasacommons/albums/72157634975233898. As a participating institution on The Commons Flickr website, NASA for various reasons has determined that "no known copyright restrictions" exist for images that are posted to the NASA on The Commons Flickr web page. In addition, an independent analysis of applicable law was accomplished before proceeding with the particular use of NASA on The Commons Hubble Space Telescope images for use in *Our Amazing Universe* – "All About This & That" Picture Book Series for Children (Volume 2). As a result of this analysis, all NASA images used in the publication of this book were not noted by NASA as protected by copyright. In accordance with NASA's Media Usage Guidelines, "If not copyrighted, NASA material may be reproduced and distributed without further permission from NASA." See NASA's Media Usage Guidelines web page at the following link for further information -- https://www.nasa.gov/multimedia/guidelines/index.html. For further information concerning the The Commons Flickr image posting and usage guidelines, see the 'About the Rights Statement' and 'Copyright on Photographs' sections at the following link -- https://www.flickr.com/commons/usage/.

2. **Astronomy Printshop Image Gallery**, HubbleSite, STScI website -- http://hubble.stsci.edu/gallery/printshop/step1.php. The images excerpted from the HubbleSite Astronomy Printshop Image Gallery were created by the Office of Public Outreach at the Space Telescope Science Institute (STScI). The Institute has been contracted by NASA to create products and services that return the scientific discoveries of the Hubble Space Telescope to the American public. STScI created these images to be widely distributed to the general public as part of their outreach effort. To that end, STScI has released the images contained in the Astronomy Printshop Gallery into the public domain. See the STScI letter dated 1 May 2008 at the following HubbleSite link for details -- http://hubblesite.org/go/notice

Note: The image used on the front book cover of *Our Amazing Universe* is entitled, "Hubble Space Telescope Celebrates 25 Years of Unveiling the Universe" and was retrieved from NASA on The Commons Flickr web page on 28 March 2017 at https://www.flickr.com/photos/nasacommons/17124636658/in/album-72157634975233898/. Credits for all other images used in the *Our Amazing Universe* book are given proper acknowledgement underneath each of the respective pictures.

Check out more new, interesting, fun-filled volumes from the
"About This & That" Picture Book Series for Children.

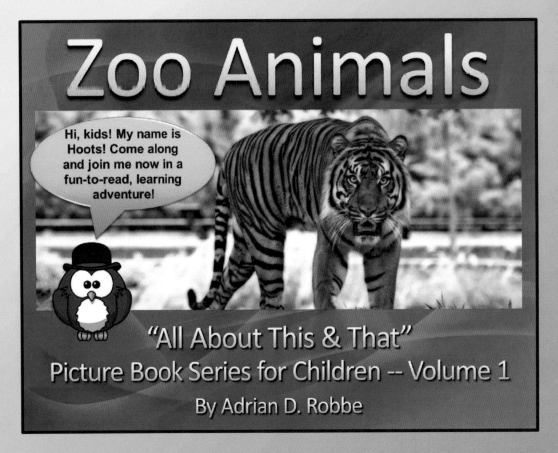